WORDY FOLKS IN A PAPER WORLD

MUSTAFA MURTUZA TOPIWALA

ISBN 979-888606239-7

I dedicate this book to my parents and my twin brother for their constant support and affection in all my endeavors, and always being by my side. I give this book as a present to myself for bringing a smile on people's face through my words, and I honor the poem within to my family and friends who have always motivated me to improve my work.

Contents

Foreword

A few comments from my beloved readers:

"Outstanding. Portrays sentiments that sound far beyond your years. These theme based ones will make a mark someday somewhere."

"Brilliant, very readable."

"Nostalgic, whimsical, pretty! Just what I needed to read."

"Heart-touching, takes anyone down the memory lane, keep it up!!"

Preface

I wrote this book as a compilation of handpicked poems that I have written over the years. All of them cover a wide range of topic, themes and emotions that have been penned down sophistically. A majority of them do not adhere to conventional poetic forms of writing, but there are no bounds to language and I have chosen to experiment with words rather than constrict myself. Motivational, jolly, sentient: I am pretty sure that at the end of this book, rich emotions will have been invoked in you and restored your trust in the power of simple, yet profound poetry.

Acknowledgements

Hussain Topiwala, for always proofreading my poems;

Zoyab Kadi uncle, for providing reliable feedback;

My mom and dad, for the support I needed.

Prologue

'All of our life's stories have unique plots, though they have flipped
to the same page today-
But we will emerge soon, look at another man's face and think,
'He was there too,' and wonder how our stories came to interlink;
We shall watch a new sun rise in the absence of a friend, parent, or
brother
And still remember we were all in this together'

1. COVID-19

Those years weren't a phase, they were a black spot in our history,

They could never be forgotten, never be expunged from our memory.

An invisible, toxic army of a gazillion soldiers took over the Earth,

We were slow to respond, but we fought for all it was worth.

Our faces masked, our hands gloved, we were caged in our concrete zoo,

While doctors, nurses, and reporters painstakingly unremembered their loved ones' rue.

With tears hidden behind safety suits, many, oh many, only watched with hands stretched out,

As pieces of their hearts were buried deep inside the earth and they could only be spectators throughout.

Streets were devoid of the games, the banter, and the laughs of children-

They had grown over time, in their longing for schools to reopen.

We attempted and crashed, but did we stop trying? No, we never did.

Fathers and mothers, sons and daughters, fought for each other even if the world did forbid.

Men and women lost their jobs and everything they had ever
worked for-
We were all in the same boat, the boat had set sail, but it had
washed ashore.
When we had to distance ourselves from one another,
When we couldn't hold hands and pray together,
Did we stop trying? No, we never did. We attempted and
crashed, but tried again.
All of our life's stories have unique plots, though they have
flipped to the same page today-
But we will emerge soon, look at another man's face and
think,
'He was there too,' and wonder how our stories came to
interlink;
We shall watch a new sun rise in the absence of a friend,
parent, or brother
And still remember we were all in this together.

2. SOMETIMES

Sometimes, when it showers during the summer,
Rain that washes beads of sweat
And ignites joy amidst all the slumber,
The horrid heat had beset.
Sometimes, when fate by chance
Lets you stumble across
A soul you thought
Forever you had lost.
Sometimes, when you find that toy-
Torn and worn to shreds and strings,
And yet it helps you remember the boy
Whose imagination had been gifted wings.
Sometimes, when the smell of tea
Fills you one day, and your lips
Curve into a smile, wondering,
When did coffee become everyday's trip?
Sometimes, when the stars shine
Ever so brighter than the moon,
You forget you were 'bout to whine
And instead begin to croon.
Sometimes, when your fingers run
Through the pages of your comfort book
And wish, with heavy glee, the story could have begun

Once more, and tread the lane it had once took.
Sometimes, it feels great to stop
Amidst the chaos that rocks lives,
Heave a sigh and merrily drop
Down into our old drives.
Sometimes, it helps to rent-
When we have lost the way to live,
A smile, be whatever the moment
And relive the days, never-ending we believed.
Sometimes it's best to remember
How to live our forgotten lives,
Stoke the fire of the dying ember
Aid the inner self to revive, sometimes.

3. COLOURS

It is really impossible to
Imagine a fresh color
That no one has seen-
Something new;
When to each passing day
There are, and will be
The same hues-
What's the point anyway?
The point of the routine?
Of winning, and losing, sometimes:
What's meant to be, has already been;
The struggle, the path-
Both might be different
Yet the goal is
Relatively the same.

Then said the wingman raven
At his shoulder-
'My nest on the conifer
Isn't the safest haven.
A storm? A predator!
No, the very-homely branches
Aren't permanent!

The goal may be similar
But the destination isn't-
It's how you see the same colors differently
that changes it.
Each road is different:
I gaze from the heights of my nest-
A new color is right there,
You just haven't seen it yet!'

4. COMMUNITY

I was one among the thousand
Men and women in my village;
A tiny group of humans, a small
branch amidst the world's foliage.

Our habits and our lives were twined-
Strangers called us a 'community,'
But we knew better than that,
We were closer than a family.

Hand-in-hand, side-by-side,
We stood by each other-
If a fist clenched in silent pain,
The village would be in it together.

I was brimmed with pride-
Our strong solidarity
Only grew stronger each time
In any adversity –

Until a dark storm whirled in from the abyss-
The ghastly pit of human evil,
Blew away lives and hearts

And many were bewitched by the Devil.

Most folded their hands to protect themselves-
Eventually, so did the rest.
I only observed with empty palms
As they tried to do what they thought was best.

The branch thinned down to a twig,
When people forgot their deeper roots.
The tiny group became smaller, it
had become something none could refute.

And I for one had stood still
Throughout the unforeseen,
My mind wanted to give in-
But I had already died within.

The storm from Hell had caused destruction-
Maybe the storm was inside them
And our family made no sense,
It was evident something had changed-
The great community had lost its eminence.

5. MOULDING DREAMS

A world made of gault would seem

To be an impossible dream;

Clay people, you and me,

Who are sculpted till eternity.

We are moulded tough and strong:

To harness the wind, emerge from the throng.

Shattered to shreds; our fates - a scrawl.

We break, but do not fall.

The Earth weighs down on our backs

Yet we build ourselves from the scraps.

Clay people, you and me,

We strive to make dreams reality.

6. CONQUER

Frail bones can be broken
Quite simply with a blow,
Unless your thoughts are woven
To be the master of your woe.
Where you bridge the cleft
Between your aim, and self-doubt,
And you're not burdened under the latter's heft
As you cross the divide throughout.
When you know it is
You; against the world's grime,
And you still tread with strong steps,
Leaving your prints in the sands of time.

7. DESIRES & SATIATION

What is most satiable?
Is it the mind, the body,
Or the soul?
Is it to seek all knowledge;
Attaining an endless ataraxia,
Or gaining the materialistic bounties
One always craves to possess?
The trio seems never to replete,
As we climb to the apex of our dreams,
But the climb never ends, as dreams
Grow ceaselessly, when finally,
The mortal seeker has to depart;
Knowing, as he was never fully able to water and
Nurture the seed of desires sown in his mind.

8. THE CAGED BIRD

Hey man! Don't you see?
I am caged, please set me free!
Oh stop flashing that camera's light,
It keeps me awake all night.
Don't you like watching us dance and sing.
It will be a sight, only if you let me out of this thing.
Please, my so-called caretaker will shortly arrive.
And to make me fly through his rings, he will strive.
But I will not pass through his rings,
And why should I? I have no freedom to spread my wings.
Hey man! They say you beings are priceless.
And what am I, for they have bought and caged me for a price
so less!
All day long I remain perched and wonder why,
Why I am not permitted to fly?
And meet my kith and kin in the sky,
The sky that is free for all.
I dream of making my own nests in trees so tall.
And to find new places in a forest,
Then dance in the rain when nature is at its best.
Ah! But today I know it is my last day,
For my breath is slipping away.
For no crime I was put behind bars.

And I thought while I gazed at the stars,

It is not me who is going to mourn, because

Hey man! It is your loss.

9. WORLD THROUGH A CRAB

Peculiar, enigmatic, yet beautiful
Is the perspective of the world
Through the eyes of a tiny crab
As it traverses rocks, crawls over dunes,
Continuing its journey on the path,
A path, travelled by many creatures before
Although never looking at the path itself
As it scuttles sideways,
Trusting it's instinct to reach
Where the path takes it,
Eyes always forward, feet on the move
It does not know where it is headed,
Yet is certain of where it wishes to be.

10. VICTORIOUS, YET DEFEATED

O Comrades! The war is done.

All enmity shall banish, we have won.

O Comrades! Never forget what this victory cost.

Never fail to remember the brave souls we have lost.

O Comrades! This victory isn't achieved by luck so sheer.

No act of bravery displayed is conceived as mere.

O Comrades! Every tear was worthy shed.

But there is no ground left without a stain of red.

O Comrades! Then what is the outcome?

Surely of brutality we have set an epitome.

O Comrades! Then alas we are defeated.

Our thoughts and conscience has deceived us,

It has diverted us from the right trail,

Which is by itself is opposite to what we hail.

O Comrades! Peace, entirely will clear us from all our sins.

Only then we are true soldiers and victorious by all means.

11. INNOCENT MAN

The innocent man discovered fire,
Needs were transcended by desire.
He found multiple ways
To domesticate the wild, and strays.
Relentlessly pursuing,
His own well-being.
The innocent man began to cut trees,
And even managed to harness the breeze.
He erected huge abodes,
Cleared forests for dull roads.
To satisfy his hunger he began to feast
On all creatures, and slaughtered beasts.
Stood up factories and industries:
But his desires never seemed to cease.
Every action of his defiled the Earth,
He realized of resources there will be a dearth.
For the near end, he tried hard to save,
But the innocent man had already dug his grave.

12. WE KNOW

We know you are up there, watching from your golden castle;
As we sweat and toil, trudge and bleed, to get through the hustle.
Some of us struggle to live, yet all of us are in a quiet strife-
We know you live off bit by bit on our life.
You were chosen, remember? By people who trusted you,
Who thought they would live to see a better avenue.
We know there was no right choice in the game;
It did not matter who won, the outcome was always meant to be the same-
Broken roads, broken houses, broken countries, broken world,
We know we are mired in a place that you deserved.
All those silenced protests still echo within us,
Yet you never accepted your mistakes without a fuss.
We know you watch the sun rise from your golden castle
As we carry it on our backs, and get through the hustle.
Draconian laws, dodgy moves, anything to fuel the selfish yeast and get the dough
We chose you. We are watching too, we know.

13. BOOKS

As a small boy he wanted to learn
The ways and terms of the world;
And thus he read a plethora of books
To get an idea of what it looks.
Through the pages and words he read,
With thoughts of authors his mind was fed -
A world of dragons, castles and knights;
Of elves, fairies, and many other delights.
With plenty more pages turned,
An idea in his brain wormed.
In mirth he decided to embark on a journey -
To embrace a world nothing short of ecstasy.
A short moment later, he realized he would need money,
And search for a grown up who would accompany.
He could not cover the world on foot,
The size of his expedition he clearly mistook.
Probably dragons weren't affable,
Or elves weren't cute and dainty, rather laughable.
After all, he was quite a little boy,
Who knows, the world might be a decoy.
He picked up a book and plunged into its words -
And immersed himself in different worlds.